Never Be Ordinary

Never Be Ordinary
Wisdom from My Father

by
John Cusick

In Honor of
George L. Cusick

Never Be Ordinary

Copyright © 2018 by John Cusick

10 9 8 7 6 5 4 3 2

ISBN 978-1-7321150-2-6

Published by
Corby Books
A Division of Corby Publishing LP
P.O. Box 93
Notre Dame, Indiana 46556

Manufactured in the United States of America

Dedicated to George and Florence Cusick,
ordinary parents who raised their kid well.

"*And now the old man's gone
And I'd give all I own
To hear what he said when I wasn't listening
To my old man.*"

– Steve Goodman

CONTENTS

Seminal Moments

AS I LOOK BACK ON MY LIFE, I have come to recognize a few seemingly insignificant moments that had a profound effect on the way I think, look at life, make decisions, shape my beliefs, and continue to direct the remaining years of my life.

I have come to realize that these brief encounters, when a sentence or two was spoken to me, have profoundly shaped my decisions and practices throughout my life.

The seminal moments within these pages did not jump out of the pages of any book, nor were they proclaimed in a classroom setting. They were not uttered by popular preachers or inspirational speakers.

Each one was spoken during the first quarter of my life by the least likely person—my dad.

And each of these seminal moments occurred in the course of daily conversation—around the kitchen table, in the neighborhood tavern (yes, kids were allowed to hang out there in those days), at the ballpark, in the family car, and in letters from "home." Some of these seminal moments were quickly dismissed, and yet somehow these little sound bites in the midst of larger conversations pierced the thick veneer of my teenaged and twenty-something self and stayed in the deep recesses of my mind and memory.

The seminal moment that transformed my dad's seemingly ordinary words into the driving force in my life occurred late in the afternoon on Wednesday, September 22, 1971. My father died.

Even though everything looked the same, I was beginning a process of seeing and experiencing everything differently. The death of someone with whom you have a very special bond rooted in love always has the possibility of changing so much in life. It did for me and maybe it did or will for you.

How many times in the first quarter of my life did I read and hear the words of St. Paul: "In the end there are three things that last: faith, hope and love. And the greatest of these is love." Now, in the ninth month of 1971, I was beginning to realize what that meant.

As I began to retrieve those moments and experiences I lived with my dad, and began to reflect on the profound effect each one has had and continues to have on me, I discovered that they are not unique to me. In each of the stories in this little book of wisdom from my dad, you too might find the same truths and values I have. The author of each one is unique to my life as are the circumstances and the wording. But there is a really good chance they will resonate with you and your life experience.

I am a person of Faith and a Catholic Priest by chosen profession. I have discovered that each of these pieces of wisdom from my dad is rooted in the stories of my Faith. They really are spiritual stories with a big "S" and a small "s."

I write these reflections for several reasons:

1. I want to honor my father (and mother, too!). That is what my Faith commands Me to do: "Honor thy father and mother."

2. I want to share with you how the comments from a very ordinary man, and in hindsight an extraordinary father, changed my behavior, enhanced my faith, and

transformed me into a far better son, priest, and person than I could have been on my own.

3. I hope these reflections might unlock seminal moments and tidbits of wisdom in your own life. Some might make you smile. Others might cause a lump in your throat or water in your eyes.

May you discover the sacred within you.

In our Sacred Scripture in the book of Genesis, we read that Yahweh God breathed into the nostrils of Adam the breath of life. And the man came alive. I finally see the parallel!

These quotes and experiences were breathed into me by my dad. Many stayed deep within for many years. Gradually I became aware of what was breathed into me, and I, too, came to life in ways I never could have imagined.

"Never be ordinary, John, if you ever have the opportunity to be someone special."

INTRODUCTION

BY THE STANDARDS OF THE WORLD, I had a very ordinary dad. He died too young after living an ordinary, non-descript life.

But something quite remarkable happened as I grew older. My dad became a wisdom figure in my life. His oddities, weaknesses, quirks, mistakes, problems and deficiencies were transfigured into life lessons that he bestowed on me, his only child.

Though my dad has been dead longer than I ever knew him alive, I am the recipient of some amazing common-sense wisdom from father to son. He told me each one of these recollections when he was alive but, at the time I heard them, they were in one ear and out the other. Ah, the genius of a know-it-all teenager! However, they remained somewhere in the deep recesses of my mind and memory. Thank God!

I have recalled each one of these "sound bites" in this book after my dad had died. Though I have thanked him over and over again "in spirit," I never had the chance to thank him face-to-face during the almost 26 years I had him in my life on this earth. And here's what's equally important: I never had a good conversation with my dad about these great pieces of inherited wisdom and profound insights into life. He died when I was too young and self-centered to realize his brilliance.

But even if he had lived longer, I am quite certain we probably never would have had such a conversation. He wasn't much of a talker, and I wasn't much of a listener…then.

After all, he was just an ordinary dad!

George L. Cusick, 1912–1971

I know very little about my dad's growing-up years. He talked very little about those years in his life, and I didn't ask. Only once or twice did he speak about his own father, who died before I was born. I believe my grandfather worked for the Chicago Transit Authority (CTA) as a motorman on the streetcars. I concluded from whispers in the extended family that he most likely died of the "creature." That was the name many Irish used to speak of the dreaded disease of alcoholism. It was no disease in those days, but rather a family embarrassment that was never talked about in the Cusick family.

My dad was a member of the first graduating class of Leo High School on the Southside of Chicago. He attended only one semester of college and never told me why he dropped out, but I concluded his departure was due to the Great Depression, which began in 1929. My dad was 17 and economic survival was more important than academic success.

One day I travelled downtown to meet my dad for lunch. He worked for the Chicago, Rock Island, and Pacific Railroad. His office was in LaSalle Street Station. On the way to lunch, he pointed out where he got his first job: the Western Union Telegraph Office across the street from the train station. He literally ran telegrams to the buildings in downtown Chicago for 12 hours a day. His daily salary? $1.

He left his salaried job, went across the street and began working as a "Red Cap." He unloaded the luggage of train passengers from cars and cabs and brought the luggage to their trains.

And conversely, he unloaded people's luggage from their incoming trains and brought it to a waiting car or cab. His salary? Tips. He stayed with the railroad business until the day he died, September 22, 1971. And after 35 years of loyal service at the "Rock," he was rewarded with a third week of vacation. He was an ordinary guy with an ordinary job.

Yet in his late 20s he did a pretty adventuresome thing. He travelled a great distance by streetcar with a few of his buddies to the Northside of Chicago to a dance hall where he met a pretty woman: Florence Kauth, my mom. They married in 1943, and he took her on a long journey to the Southside of Chicago to a small apartment where I was born in 1945.

They had an ordinary marriage. Well, not really. It had some cultural oddities from the get-go. They came from foreign lands within the same city. They were as foreign and distant figuratively speaking as Baghdad is from Boston. They married outside of their ethnic tribes. An Irish-English guy married a woman of German ancestry. It was a mixed marriage! That was very unusual for the mid-1940s.

And my dad had married an older woman—mom was eight years my dad's senior. She was tagged as the "old German" by my dad's overbearing family. I learned it was not a term of endearment. It was a term used to talk about her in a derogatory manner, but, of course, never to her face!

My mom told me that my dad did not have a penny to his name when they got married. But she did. As a matter of fact, she had quite a few pennies. For a number of years, she was a single working woman for Sears, Roebuck and Company. She participated in the company's profit-sharing plan. She saved every penny.

My dad married up! He married an older, pretty woman who had socked away some money. It was that money that allowed them to buy a three-flat, and eight years later a single-family house. My dad could never have done that on his salary from his ordinary job.

It was inside the walls of our third-floor apartment in the three-flat and later inside the small two-story, three-bedroom house that the wisdom of my father was passed on to me.

"Jump in. I'll watch out for you."

"Never turn down an opportunity."

"If I were him, I wouldn't fight for then either."

"Are you OK?"

"I always admired those who didn't smoke."

"Try hard."

"Never be ordinary, if you ever have the opportunity to be someone special."

What follows are my remembrances of those pieces of wisdom and how they continued to be applied in my life. These remembrances have made me a better person.

George Cusick was an ordinary guy with a great amount of extraordinary wisdom. I only wish he could have lived longer, and I could remember more of his wisdom.

But what I remember, I am delighted to pass on to you.

CHAPTER

1

___

"Jump in. I'll watch out for you"

AROUND THE AGE OF 9 OR 10, I discovered swimming and adventure—both at the same time. I was a real urban kid.

I lived in an apartment building until age five and then transitioned to a three-flat with a cement backyard. There was not a lot of green space. There was an alley behind our garage, and that, too, was concrete. As little kids we played baseball in that alley. Two sewer covers were home and second base. The two other bases were downspouts from the gutters of our neighbors' garage and our garage.

When we got bicycles, we would ride them to school, two blocks away, and to the store, three blocks away.

As an urban kid, that was pretty much my world. I don't think I was ever at a beach or a lake.

However, adventure was about to begin! My friend John and I discovered there was an indoor swimming pool at Ridge Park, but the park was about two-and-a-half miles away from our neighborhood. That seemed about as far from the Southside of Chicago as Montana. Urban kids stayed in their own neighborhoods.

However, we came up with an idea. How about asking our moms if we could ride our bikes to the pool? We asked. They said yes! Off we went with our swimming suits wrapped up in towels.

Can you imagine that today? Two ten-year-old kids, riding bicycles two-and-a-half miles by themselves? Nope. No way.

We were in that pool nearly every day during that summer. We had a blast each and every day.

One Saturday, while John and I were splashing around in the shallow end of the pool, my dad showed up. Parallel to the pool was a small spectator section. When I saw my dad, I leapt out of the pool to say hello.

"John, why are you and John in the shallow end of the pool?"

"We don't know how to swim."

"Come on down to the other end of the pool."

"You mean the deep end?"

"Yes. Follow me."

In the spectator section my dad walked to the other end. I followed along the side of the pool.

"John, now jump in."

3

"Jump in? I can't. It's over my head!"

"Just jump in along the side of the pool. Then come straight up and grab the top."

"Are you sure?"

"Jump in. I'll watch out for you."

I stared at the water, afraid of what might happen to me. Then, all of a sudden, I jumped in. I could feel nothing under my feet. As a matter of fact, that was the first time in my life there was nothing under my feet. It was weird and scary.

I shot right back up and grabbed the side of the pool. The length of that experience? No more than five seconds.

I made it! I didn't drown!

"How was that, John?"

"Weird!" There was nothing under my feet. But I did it.

"Now this time jump out about three feet. When you come up for air, come back to the side of the pool. I'll watch you."

4

I popped back up to the top of the water and scrambled as fast as I could to the side of the pool. Maybe nine seconds.

Then it was six feet. Then 15 feet. Soon it was half the width of the pool. And by the end of the free-swim hour I made it all the way across to the other side.

Each new adventure came with the same mantra from my dad: "I'll watch out for you."

It was so neat that soon I forgot that nothing was under my feet. And I felt safe. My dad kept reminding me, "I'll watch out for you."

When the lifeguards blew the whistle signaling the end of the swim period, I was wearing my swimsuit and an enormous smile. I went right over to where my dad was standing. It was only then that I realized that between the two of us was a chain-link fence that ran from floor to ceiling between the pool and the spectator section.

I never saw the fence. I only saw my dad.

I never heard all the noise of kids in the pool. I only heard my dad's voice: "John, I'll watch out for you." If he wanted to help, protect, or save me, he couldn't. There was a barrier.

But there was no barrier between my dad and me. I saw his care and his protective love for me.

I was a little scared at first, but when I heard him say, "I'll watch out for you," I knew he would take care of me. What fence?

There is a word for that experience I learned later on: *trust*. In that pool, even with a fence between us, I had complete and total trust in my dad. He would watch me. He would watch over me. He would not let harm come my way.

Oh, I had some fear and I got scared on occasion, but I never lost trust in my dad. He would invite me to do things I thought I never could do, and take me to places I never would have gone on my own. He led. I followed. He was my dad.

6

I was a very lucky kid. And for the next 15 years I never doubted that trust.

As an adult, I learned the antithesis of trust: *suspicion*.

My small world of trust has given way to a larger world of suspicion. Suspicion seems to pervade almost every aspect of modern life.

Suspicion runs very high between races, religions, political parties, nations, the media, politicians, the haves and have-nots, and between generations. Too many of us will only see the fence.

Yet, in the midst of my crazy adult world I can still hear him say to me, "Jump in. I'll watch out for you."

I did. He did, too. I pray he still does.

This particular episode brought to mind a very early memory in my life. I remember the very first prayer that my parents taught me:

"Angel of God, my guardian dear,
To whom God's love commits me here,

Ever this day be at my side,
To light, to guard, to rule, to guide.
Amen."

Sometimes guardian angels look like dads.

CHAPTER

2

"Never turn down an opportunity"

I RAN HOME. I was scared.

I wasn't scared of anything bad. On the contrary, I was afraid of something potentially good.

Isn't it funny how good news is often met with fear?

Think about popping the Big Question: Will you marry me? Can we spend the rest of our lives together? Even if you have been waiting to ask or waiting to answer such questions, after the initial positive response something happens between our ears. It becomes an "O My God" moment.

Fear can trump all that joy. "Is this right?" "Is this the right person?" "Can we make it last?" "What happens if it fails?"

Likewise—when it comes to starting a family of your own—you have dreamed of being a parent. The results have come back. You will be having a baby. It is one of those "O My God" moments! How exciting! The tears of utter joy are rolling down your face.

And yet in a little while..."Will the child be healthy?" "Is it right to bring a child into this pain-filled, crazy world?" "Can I be an effective parent?" Fear.

"John, I want you to be my assistant," said Ed Barr, the caddy master at Beverly Country Club.

Me? He must be mistaken. I was only 15 years old. I was only in my second year as a caddy. I was small of stature. There were about 200 caddies who were older than me, bigger than me, and stronger than me. As Ed's assistant, I would be their boss!

All the data was saying that I could not or should not be the Assistant Caddy Master at the prestigious BCC, Beverly Country Club.

I suppose the look of fear on my face said it all. "John, go home and think about it. You can let me know tomorrow."

It was probably the most afraid I had ever felt in my young life. And what triggered my reaction? A fear of something bad? No. It was a fear of something good—an opportunity! Good news triggered a fearful reaction. I was not being offered a job. I was being offered a promotion. There was only one Assistant Caddy Master position. It was being offered to a 15-year-old kid with limited experience. Some of the members' golf bags were bigger and seemed to weigh more than this little caddy!

I didn't walk home that day after caddying. I ran home! Fear had given me new energy.

"Dad," I said as I ran into the kitchen, "Ed Barr wants me to be his assistant. What should I do?"

Unknowingly, I became the poster boy for the definition of a 15-year-old teenager: a sophisticated young adult capable of making life decisions by himself one minute; the needy, insecure kid asking his parent for help, decision-making, and wisdom the next minute. And if my dad said, "Take the job," and it didn't work out, I would blame him. Ah, the genius of adolescence.

So I waited at the kitchen table for my dad to answer my question. And answer he did, but with an answer I didn't expect. It was an answer that I have employed to this very day in my 70s. His answer to a simple question was transformed into a life strategy:

"John, never turn down an opportunity."

What?! That doesn't answer my question. C'mon, dad! Just tell me—should I say yes or no to the invitation to become the Assistant Caddy Master at Beverly Country Club!?

Never turn down an opportunity.

It was more than an answer to a particular question or situation. My dad was offering me a strategy that I could use throughout my life. And I have done just that, even in retirement.

Why did I react with fear? Instead of seeing Ed Barr's invitation as an opportunity, I reacted to it with all the reasons why I could not do it. I was too young. I was too small. I lacked experience. I had never been a leader. So many other kids in the caddy yard were better suited than me to be the Assistant Caddy Master to such a well-known guy as Ed Barr. I was afraid of the change—in my role and responsibility, and in the way I saw myself.

The next morning I returned to the

Country Club and told the Caddy Master I would take the job. I still had all my misgivings of age, experience, size, talent and more, but after thinking about the job offer and my dad's counsel I was now aware of something new and exciting. It was an opportunity.

In the course of the next four-and-a-half years, I was the Assistant Caddy Master at BCC.

My dad's response opened wide my mind, and especially my imagination.

Never turn down an opportunity. What a fascinating way to look at decision-making. How often do we make key decisions based on fear: "What if I am not good enough or qualified enough to do that?" "What if this might happen or that might happen?"

We turn down opportunities based upon possible mistakes and possible failures we might make.

And, of course, there is always the financial

lens that is used to assess an opportunity. "Will I be offered enough money?"

In the end, there really is only one question: "Am I being offered an opportunity?"

Never turn down an opportunity.

Opportunity is not a guarantee. It is a risk. It is taking a chance. It is the possibility of failure. But it is also the hope of great success.

It's talking you into something, rather than talking yourself out of something.

Since that encounter with my dad at the kitchen table, the list of opportunities to which I have said yes can fill several pages. I am a much better person, a more complete person and a smarter person because I have said "Yes."

After more than three years of retirement and living out my early 70s, other opportunities have arisen, including coming out of my comfort zone and writing this book. How do you think I responded?

Thanks, dad.

3

"If I were him, I wouldn't fight for them either"

MY DAD WAS A PRODUCT OF HIS TIMES. But aren't we all? He was not a social leader, neither was he a mindless follower. He was an ordinary Southside Chicago guy. One of the issues that was a part of his life was the race question. Then and now Chicago has been defined as one of the most segregated cities in America. We lived in a black-and-white world. Or more honestly, we, our family, lived in a white world.

Integration on the Southside of Chicago was defined as that short period of time from when the first black family moved in until the last white family moved out. In the taverns where my dad would have a beer with others, there were two primary topics of conversation: sports and "how far are 'they' getting in our neighborhoods?"

"Race relations" was not a big topic of conversation in our home, but it wasn't ignored either. It was a normal part of our conversation. I was led to believe from what I heard at home and from those times my dad took me to the tavern with him that black people were a threat to our neighborhood and to our way of life. I imagined them as an enemy army moving from east to west. The possibility in those days of a mixed-race neighborhood was out of the question. I did not know a single African-American person until I began high school in the fall of 1958.

In 1964 Cassius Clay changed his name to Muhammad Ali and his religion to Islam. In 1966 at the pinnacle of his professional boxing career he announced that he would not sign up for the draft, which could possibly lead him into the army and into the Vietnam War.

Somewhere between that time and April 1967 when Ali was arrested for refusing to be drafted into the military, an amazing thing happened to me courtesy of my dad.

Cassius Clay was always a controversial figure in our neighborhood. He was an arrogant, loud-mouthed braggart who happened to be very good at his craft: boxing. But now that Muhammad Ali was a draft dodger, he became one of the most hated people in our neighborhood and beyond. He might be a great boxer but, as a draft dodger, he was un-American.

Amazingly, in the midst of this situation my dad, sitting at the kitchen table, uttered this piece of wisdom:

"John, if I were him, I wouldn't fight for them either. After all, what have we done for those people, and now we want them to fight our wars."

Wow! My dad said what?!

I was stunned. I could never imagine my dad taking the side of Muhammad Ali. Never. As I mentioned, he was not a leader in the area of social issues. But he was not a blind follower of the status quo either. Yet this was the most "liberal" comment I had ever heard him make.

When I began to think about it, my dad was driven by common sense, not by ideology. And his comment about Muhammad Ali, once I thought about it, made sense. It made good common sense. Dad assessed the state of affairs among many black people living in America, and realized that their chance for social opportunity or their ability to inherit the American dream was very limited. "And we want them to fight 'our' wars?" How telling.

Something else occurred within me as a result of my dad's comment. I was having an awakening. The genie was slowly coming out of the bottle. I was beginning to look at the same things I saw and experienced differently. If my dad could say it, I could do it.

In many ways those two sentences weren't as much a social commentary on the times, but an inspiring statement directed at me. I saw it as my time to re-examine so many things and evaluate my values, dreams, and ideals.

We were living in exciting, yet turbulent, times. The mid-sixties were the post-President Kennedy years, the Vietnam War, civil protests across the country, the assassinations of a president-hero, a black prophet, and the president-hero's brother. For those of us who were Catholic, it was the time of Pope John XXIII and the Second Vatican Council.

My critical judgment was unleashed. My idealism for country and Church was defining me. What could be—and not the status quo—was propelling me forward.

Oh, the times they were a-changing!

To this day I do not believe I was influenced as much by a changing culture, the thoughts of teachers and classmates, books, articles, newspapers, radio and television commentaries as much as I was by my family values spoken by my dad, supported by my mom, and lived out by the three of us.

I was more influenced by the fact that my dad was so excited that Catholic Mass was now celebrated in English than I was by any priest or liturgy course in the seminary.

I kept returning to his comment. "John, if I were him [Ali], I wouldn't fight for them either. After all, what have we done for those people, and now we want them to fight our wars." And the more I reflected on what he said, the more I came to realize that people were more important than systems, government, institutions, and that time-honored mantra: "That's the way it's always been." Cultural systems, government, business and religions now seemed to me as "sacred" only because they had been around for a long time. Once I took a deeper look, what they did and how they affected life was far from "sacred." That was an important epiphany for me.

And because of dad and all that was going on inside of me and all around me in my country, my Church, and God's world, I developed a new mantra: "People before programs."

I now began to evaluate almost everything from this perspective.

At another time my dad said something to the effect that our family and neighborhood doesn't need much from the government after security and basic services. It is the poor and the disadvantaged that he believed needed the government the most.

And who continues to get screwed out of good education, health care, nutrition, jobs, opportunities, security and basic services? You got it. It's the same old same old, the poor and everyone else at the bottom of the social ladder.

My first Pastor, Fr. Bill Clark, said it another way: "Nearly everyone in our country has some group lobbying for their needs, except the poor. The poor have no voice. It is our religious institutions that need to step up and be the voice and lobby for the poor. Find where the poor are and you will see where Christ is."

I never realized at that time how much a two-sentence statement could open the door inside of me to so much. But it did and it still does. What have we done for those people, and we expect them to fight our wars? People before programs. What can you do for your country? When you figure that out, you will see where Christ is.

I have been—and continue to be—called many things. The most revealing might have been a comment that one Cardinal Archbishop of Chicago quipped about me, "Oh, he's one of the '60s priests." Cardinal, I am not a fad-priest tied to a past era.

If you want to call me anything, please call me a son of my father. And I have two fathers, George Cusick and God, my everloving Father. Call me the son of either one, the other won't mind.

CHAPTER

4

___

"Are you OK?"

DURING SEMESTER BREAK ONE WINTER I had two auto accidents in an hour and a half. Neither was serious. Each was a fender bender, but accidents nonetheless. I was driving the family car. It was the only car we owned.

On a very icy side street I slid into an oncoming car. The headlight sections of both cars met each other. Both cars seemed drivable. The police were called and an accident report was filled out. I exchanged my name and address information with the other driver.

I called my mom while the report was being filled out.

"Mom, I had a minor car accident."

"Oh, John, are you OK? Is everyone else OK?"

"Everybody is fine."

With all the paperwork completed, I got back in the car and continued my journey home. I got to the end of the same side street and I slid into another oncoming car! This fender bender took out the other headlight and front fender. Everyone in both cars was fine. I was a wreck! I had never had an auto accident during my short duration as a driver. And now within 90 minutes I had two.

The police were called. I was praying fervently that the same policeman would not appear at the scene of this accident! I got lucky. It was a different police officer. I called my mom a second time. Before I could say a single word, mom said, "John, are you on your way home?"

"Yes, but I had another accident." I think I heard the phone fall to the floor.

"Oh John, are you sure you are OK?"

"Yes, mom, I am OK, but the front end of the car is a mess. But I can drive it home."

I was OK on the outside, but I could feel myself shaking on the inside. When I got behind the steering wheel, I became a white-knuckle driver with both hands tightly gripping the steering wheel. I was driving about five miles per hour! The last thing I wanted to do was drive that car or any car ever again.

I parked the car right in front of our house. When I opened the door, I was greeted by my dad. I was really worried about facing him and having to explain how I trashed our only car. He put his arms around me tightly and said,

"*Are you OK?*"

I expected a stern look, but I got a tight hug.

"John, you are probably very tired. Why

don't you go up to bed? We can deal with this in the morning." I did.

When morning came, my dad was waiting for me in the living room. My stomach was in a knot. I looked out the small window in the front door. Our car was not there. In its place was my aunt's car.

"John, I need to go to the store. Why don't you drive me?" And he handed me the keys to my aunt's car. I, who never wanted to drive again, got behind the wheel of the car and drove the five or six blocks to the store.

From that moment until the day that he died, he never mentioned those two accidents. Never.

His only concern was me, not the car.

"Are you OK?"

He taught me a great lesson from that experience. The past is never coming back. Don't dwell on it. Let it go. Face the future. No need to dwell on the past.

I think he realized I was doing a pretty good job of beating myself up and replaying those accidents over and over again in my head. He saw no need to pile on. But he saw a big need to reassure me that I was OK.

I was OK to drive again.

I was OK to face the future.

I was OK to learn from what happened.

I was OK to let it go.

And, most importantly, I was OK in his eyes. He was my dad. I was his son. Nothing would diminish that fact—even a little.

I learned that there are three moments in life: the past, the present, and the future. The past is gone, never to return. The present moment just ended. So, all that remains is everything that lies ahead: the future.

It's such a valuable life skill to keep our eyes on the prize, not on the skeletons in our closet.

My dad wanted me to focus on where

I was going, not where I had been. Oh, yes, learn from "what was," but there is no need for "what was" to hold any of us hostage. We are free to face the future, not be paralyzed by our past.

And if we can implement that strategy in our own lives, then we need to make sure we implement that strategy in all of our relationships, whether they are personal, business, family, or social.

There is no need to remind people of the negative aspects of their past—even humorously. In what we may see as funny in a past experience with someone else, there is always a sliver of truth that may seem small to us, but huge in the memory of the other person. Just let it go.

If we can do that, I am convinced we can have a healthier family, a much better work environment, and our relationships will be built on love and mutual respect.

There is really no need to beat up people by making them relive memories of past experiences.

But there is a great need to make sure others are OK, and then get behind the wheel of that proverbial car, put it in gear, and drive forward.

5

"I always admired those who didn't smoke"

I HAVE AN ASHTRAY on a shelf of one of my bookcases. It has not been used in many, many years. It has become a symbol sacred to me and to no one else. Each time I see it is a reminder of two things: what I did for love on September 25, 1971, and something my father said to me about 10 years earlier.

I began smoking during a class retreat while in high school. There was a little store inside the retreat house where you could buy gum, candy, chips, aspirin and cigarettes. It was on the honor system. So, I placed my money in the collection box and picked out my first pack of cigarettes and a book of matches. I went outside and walked to an isolated place on the retreat house grounds and lit up a cigarette. Yuk! I tried to inhale and I thought my eyeballs were about to pop out of my head as I began coughing.

I kept at it until I began to enjoy smoking. By September 25, 1971, I was smoking two-and-a-half packs of Newport Menthol cigarettes every day.

I did not tell my parents that I was a smoker. I hid my cigarettes in the bottom right drawer of the desk in my bedroom. You would have to be quite an inspector to find them.

Mom found them.

Holding up a pack, she said, "I see you have taken up smoking." That was obvious.

No need for me to expound on that data. I knew what was to come. She would be on the phone to my dad at work to relay the evidence she had uncovered.

I wasn't looking forward to our dinner conversation that night. All day I wondered how my dad would handle this smoking situation. He was a heavy smoker and mom smoked for a number of years before she quit.

Once again, my dad said the unexpected!

"John, I have always admired those who didn't smoke."

No monologue on the rightness or wrongness of smoking. No insight into the growing health concerns about cigarettes. He took it to a different and higher level.

He did not offer a legal response or a medical response to my smoking, but a virtuous response: admiration.

On so many key issues in my young life, he once again caught me off guard. I always admired those who didn't do what you and I do.

We both smoked. He smoked Chesterfield regular cigarettes for 37 years. It was cigarette smoking that caused his death at age 59 on September 22, 1971.

Three weeks prior to that date, he lost his voice. Mom and I attributed the loss of his voice to laryngitis. The doctor said that if it didn't begin to get better in three weeks, dad would enter the hospital so that the docs could figure out what was going on. He entered the hospital on September 17 and died five days later of complications due to lung cancer.

My dad had paralyzed vocal chords and a tumor so large in his lung that removing it was not possible.

Mom and I got a call from the hospital asking us to return. My dad had taken a serious turn for the worse. By the time we arrived at Room 525, my dad had already died.

I could feel explosions in my brain. I was not ready for this. I was not prepared.

I remember clearly what I said to myself at that moment. I put my hand on my dad's forehead. And depending upon if the glass is half empty or half full, with hand on his head I could feel warmth leave or cold set in. It was dramatic and quick, and for me, scary.

I said to myself, "Dad, I will never be able to talk to you again." I felt my knees buckle. It was the first time in my life the word "never" meant never. Death is so final. No deals or compromises work. Never meant never.

Mom and I had to begin the process of preparing all the burial rites for my dad.

But something was going on inside my head that I could not share with anyone—not even my mom. There was a sudden urge to do something in the name of my dad that would be a statement of my deep love for him. It needed to be a personal thing between my dad and me.

I came to a decision about that "something" on the morning of my dad's funeral. It was something that I really didn't want to do, but I needed to do.

"John, I always admired those who didn't smoke."

That evening about 9:15, I put out my last cigarette in that ashtray that is now on my bookcase shelf. I have never smoked since then.

As I reflect on the activities that surrounded my dad's death, two things are happening. I can clearly picture my putting out that last cigarette in the ashtray that rests on my bookcase shelf. And a song is playing in my head: "What I Did for Love" from *A Chorus Line*.

And that is why I did it. The most difficult thing I could have done in loving remembrance of my dad was to quit smoking. I have never smoked again since the evening of September 25, 1971.

For the second time in three days, never meant never. "Dad, I will never be able to speak to you again." "Dad, I will never smoke again." I had no control over the former. I have complete control over the latter.

People soon learned that I quit smoking. And the analysis by many followed quickly and expectedly. "Cusick's dad died from lung cancer. And the day he buried his dad, he quit smoking. I'll bet it was that fear of lung cancer that caused him to quit."

My dad's reaction upon learning that I was now a smoker was not legal or medical. He took it to a higher level. His response was virtuous. "I always admired those who didn't smoke."

When my dad died from the effects of lung cancer, my reaction was not fear, but love.

Fear constrains. Love releases.

In the end there are three that remain:

faith, hope, and love. And the greatest of these is love.

I love you, dad.

CHAPTER

6

———

"Try hard"

SOON AFTER MY MOTHER DIED, I had the un-
enviable task of clearing out her apartment.
She had lived in the same space for over 29
years. And even though her apartment was
spotless and everything was in order, she had
accumulated a lot of things over the period of
three decades.

At the bottom of her closet I found a box
of letters. They were letters that my dad sent
me when I was away at school. Obviously, I
saved them and eventually they wound up
with my mom.

I pulled out one letter randomly and the last paragraph hit me right between my eyes.

> Mom tells me, John, that you will be on retreat soon and then your final exams before heading home for the summer.
> Try hard.
>   Love,
>   Mom and Dad

Try hard.

That was so my dad. Encouraging, but not demanding. Always supportive, but never pushy. Try hard. No need to be perfect. If I tried hard, he would never be disappointed in me.

I was an average student—never near the top of my class. That was never a possibility. But if I tried hard, I could be the best student (and the best person) I could be.

"Try hard." When I read that two-word sentence so many years later and many years after he died, I realized that was my dad's dream for me.

Try hard.

Who I was and who I would become was more important to him than what I could become. Priest is what I became. And though that meant a lot to him, I am quite certain that the quality of my character and a good work ethic were the more important aspects of the dreams he had for me.

In retrospect, I am sure that mantra of "try hard" was told by my father many different times and in many different ways.

I always tried hard. I still do.

When I made my final decision to be ordained a Catholic priest, I remember hearing my inner self say, "Well, if you are going to be a priest, then be the best priest you can be." Ever since then I have tried hard to be the best priest I could be.

I soon realized that so much of my life would be public speaking. And that required two very important elements: something of substance to communicate to others and a de-livery system that could inspire people. I was weak in both.

I began to seek out mentors who had something to say, a good pastoral theology, and a very inspiring and convincing way to say it. I watched them work. I listened intent-ly to their content. I observed their delivery. I tried hard to be the best preacher I could be.

In one nine-week period, I presided at 27 weddings. I must admit that I was as fresh during number 27 as I was for number one. I tried hard to always put the needs of the people before my own. It might have been my 27th wedding, but it was their first (and, hopefully, only). For me, to try hard means to always put the people first—to serve them the best that I can. I really try hard to do that. Thanks, dad.

Not too long ago there was chatter among the clergy about the fear of burning out. In other words, priests were working so hard for so many hours and so many days that they were not taking care of their own needs. I found it interesting that so many of those concerned about burning out had developed reputations as not being hard workers.

My response then and now has not changed: you cannot burn out what is not on fire. I am sure this is not unique to the priesthood.

I have been told that a critique of many younger people in today's workforce is found in the first three to five questions they often ask during an initial interview. "How much time off and how much vacation time do I get?" Try hard, folks. Pay your dues.

I am certain that if we all try hard many of our needs will be fulfilled, unless, of course, trying hard is not a value. And to many I am certain it is not.

There is no guarantee that trying hard

will get you to the top of the ladder. Most of us might not have that potential. But trying hard will be very fulfilling because it allows us to maximize our God-given talents whatever they are and however limited they may be.

Is it possible to try too hard? Of course, it is. We can overdose on anything.

In the world of sports, I tried too hard twice—in the sports of running and in golf.

I began playing golf as a teenager, and by the time I was in my twenties it was no longer a game, but a compulsion. It's not that I was playing all that much, but when I played, I became my own worst enemy. I was no longer playing golf to the best of my ability; I was playing to be the best.

I lost perspective on my dad's wisdom. I was no longer trying hard. I found myself trying too hard. He never challenged me to be perfect. And that is what I was trying to be and do on the golf course: hit every shot and roll every putt perfectly. I was becoming angry at myself way too much, when the ball didn't travel according to my expectations.

It was no longer a game. It became a job that I didn't like. I wasn't having fun any longer. So I quit playing golf for many years. If I could not enjoy the game of golf, I would not play golf until I could.

I have taken up playing golf again. And I really enjoy it. It's a game again. My score does not matter as much as the enjoyment I find on a golf course. I try to play well, as well as John Cusick can play. How I plan to hit the golf ball and how I actually hit the ball are often polar opposites, but I no longer have that internal anger I once experienced. Occasional disappointment, yes; but no more anger.

Try hard, John. But remember that it's only a game.

When I took up running, I could not imagine how anyone can find enjoyment in that "sport." It was like self-inflicted pain and suffering. But I kept trying. And then one day the transformation occurred—from pain to pleasure. I looked forward to finding time every day for lacing up those running shoes and hitting the pavement for 30-50 minutes. And I did that for many years…every day.

One day, while running, I came to the realization that there was not much pleasure in running any more. I had lost perspective. I was trying too hard to run every day. It was becoming an addiction. I had to run. So, like golf, I quit for a while. And was that ever hard! My head kept saying, "John, you've got to run." My guts and my dad were telling me, "No, you don't."

Being my best self meant ridding myself of addictive and compulsive behaviors that got in the way of pleasure, of play, of sport.

"Try hard, John. That's my advice to my only son."

But I must admit that I am worried about my dad's mantra, "Try Hard." In our society we tend to overdose on almost everything. We work too much. We work out too much, on and on. His mantra to me has been translated into "Try Harder and Harder."

From numerous sources, I hear that so many of our younger people, and at an early age, are under enormous pressure to get excellent grades in order to achieve admission into the very best high schools and into those high-pressure honors courses. An increasing number of our young people now have tutors to help them increase their potential ACT and SAT scores. By doing so they are more likely to be accepted at those highly competitive premier colleges.

But what is the price these people will pay in the long run? Is this what they really want to do, or is this the status symbol their parents want them to achieve?

Can you try too hard?

There is a professional tennis player and a professional golfer who did not have access to normal teen years and young adulthood. They attended school, and then played tennis and golf respectively every single day. Later in life they both crashed their adult lives. Their talented lives were completely out of control. They never had the opportunity to just be kids.

I was very lucky. I was only an average student with ordinary talent. I had parents who didn't push me beyond my means.

Thanks, dad, for encouraging me to try hard. In my 70s, I am still at it. I am still trying hard. And I am doing OK.

7

"Never be ordinary if you ever have the opportunity to be someone special"

THE MOST MEMORABLE AND PROFOUND piece of advice I ever received from my father is this:

"John, never be ordinary if you ever have the opportunity to be someone special."

This sentence has been the mantra of my life. And more than that, it has been the inspiration and the conscience of my life.

This single sentence has been woven into

my preaching, teaching and counseling. Disguised in various ways, it has been the advice I have given others in writing, email, text, private message, and any other form of communication.

It has also become fundamental to my religious faith. In our sacred text we read Jesus calling a few of his disciples, "Follow me, and I will make you fishers of men." My spin on that is found in the words of my dad: "Never be ordinary if you ever have the opportunity to be someone special."

The setting of where my dad spoke this sentence to me is classic George Cusick. It was in a tavern on south Western Avenue in Chicago. It was called The Green Door. To access the bar you needed to go through the front end of the store where you could purchase beer, cigarettes, wine, and hard liquor.

I remember the setting like it was yesterday. It was baseball season and the White Sox were playing a day game on Channel 9. The television was above us to the left. My dad ordered a Schlitz on draft and a shot of Hiram Walker bourbon. I got my usual—a Coke.

Between innings when the commercial came on, my dad rolled toward me on his barstool and spoke the now classic line of his life to me:

"John, never be ordinary if you ever have the opportunity to be someone special."

No insightful conversation preceded his remark, and there was no follow-up. The sentence just hung there in mid-air, like the smoke above the bar.

Dad rolled back on his barstool and sipped his Schlitz. The ballgame was back on.

It was not until a number of years later that his wisdom popped back into my mind. Somehow it was stored in my memory bank along with date, time and place.

It was during the grieving process after

I buried him that so many memories and words of his were pushed back into my consciousness.

His "never be ordinary" part of the sentence certainly was the foundation upon which his line, "Try hard" was built. There is no need to try hard if you believe your calling is to be ordinary—just one of the boys. "Never turn down an opportunity" had the very same foundation. If you see yourself as ordinary, you will seek out or experience few, if any, opportunities. Who you are might be all you ever will need to be.

I wish my dad would have told me what he meant by "ordinary" and what he meant by "special." He never did. I never asked. After he died it was up to me to figure it out.

I determined that "ordinary" meant don't be like me, your dad. Don't spend your life in a bar. Try hard not to be a run-of-the-mill guy living on the South Side working five days a week for the same company. And after 35 years of loyal service you are compensated with a third week of vacation, but with little money to enjoy a decent one.

He had no activities outside of the house and his job, and he belonged to no organizations. To me, all of this defines ordinary. Never be ordinary. Don't be like me, your dad.

"Special" at first hearing seemed more complicated. Hearing it, then and now, immediately leads me to three words: power, fame, money. Those are some of the defining characteristics of "special." I could not imagine any of them for me or for anyone in our family. And now, in my 70s, I was right!

What did he mean, if you ever have the opportunity to be someone special? I believe that is what he wanted me to be someday—someone special.

I arrived at this determination: Get out of here! Don't spend your life in a bar. There is a world larger and more exciting than your neighborhood. Don't be like your dad. Make something out of yourself. And when you do, then come back and help someone else.

For my dad, to be someone special meant to get ahead and develop your talent. Try hard. Grab those opportunities when you see them. Yet it didn't stop there.

Come back and help someone else. That was important to him because he really did not achieve that. He saw the value, but he fell short of achievement. He wanted to be more than he turned out to be. He was a good man—to me, a great man. He had a fascinating sense of humor. He made friends easily. People liked my dad. But he never felt he had the credentials to be a leader and a helper. He sold himself short.

"John, never be ordinary if you ever have the opportunity to be someone special."

Be more than me. Then help others to be more than you.

58

When I was asked at age 15 to be Assistant Caddy Master, I thought it might be OK to just be a caddy like everyone else. Ordinary.

With great fear in my heart, I said, "Yes." Never turn down an opportunity. Be someone special.

In the months before I chose to be ordained a Catholic priest, I decided that I would not just be a priest. Ordinary.

I would be the best priest I could be. Be someone special.

When I realized how vital good preaching was to my ministry, I realized it was not enough to read printed words off a page in front of a microphone. Ordinary.

As I have said before, I sought out the best preachers and public speakers to learn how cerebral ideas can be publicly communicated with passion, imagination, and transparency. Be someone special.

Having attained the social status of a priest, I was not better than anyone, but one with everyone. I would not issue moral imperatives to people and say, "*you* must…." Ordinary.

I made the conscious choice that the pronouns *us* and *we* made more sense. I began suggesting what *we* can do with *our* lives, and the behavior *we* should avoid to be the children of God. It was all of *us*. Be someone special.

I came to realize that living in a black-and-white world of rules, law, and authority was very easy. A deeply personal question was asked, and a black-and-white answer was given. Quote the law. State the rules. Ordinary.

But I soon became aware that our lives are complex, messy, and, sometimes, painful. Easy answers are not helpful to the complex experiences that happen to all of us. Legal answers are the goal. Offering pastoral strategies is a way to reach the finish line. Be someone special.

CHAPTER

8

May I ask a favor of you?

NEVER BE ORDINARY if <u>you</u> have the opportunity to be someone special. Keep in mind you are never too old or too young, too poor or too rich to be someone special. Being special doesn't depend on health, academic degrees (or lack thereof), or levels of happiness. "Special" is not a blood type or titles in front of your name or letters you can place after your name. Rather it is an attitude of adventure that allows you to help others, do exciting things and contribute to the betterment of the world.

61

You can't buy it. You must be it.

But try hard...every day.

And when any opportunity arises, go for it. Never turn down an opportunity! Very often life is a surprise and we must always be ready for unexpected opportunities.

And always keep your eyes and mind wide open. You may experience the presence of an angel...who just might resemble your dad.